YOUR KNOWLEDGE HAS VALUE

Owoseni Adebowale

Design Science and Natural Science

Evaluation of Socrates Article

GRIN Publishing

Bibliographic information published by the German National Library:

The German National Library lists this publication in the National Bibliography; detailed bibliographic data are available on the Internet at http://dnb.dnb.de .

Imprint:

Copyright © 2011 GRIN Verlag GmbH
Print and binding: Books on Demand GmbH, Norderstedt Germany
ISBN: 978-3-640-82447-2

This book at GRIN:

http://www.grin.com/en/e-book/166252/design-science-and-natural-science

GRIN - Your knowledge has value

Since its foundation in 1998, GRIN has specialized in publishing academic texts by students, college teachers and other academics as e-book and printed book. The website www.grin.com is an ideal platform for presenting term papers, final papers, scientific essays, dissertations and specialist books.

Visit us on the internet:

http://www.grin.com/

http://www.facebook.com/grincom

http://www.twitter.com/grin_com

Design and Natural Science
Evaluation of the Socrates Article

Blekinge Tekniska Högskola
Informatics Department
Karlskrona, Sweden

January 2011

Design and Natural Science: Evaluation of the Socrates Article

Adebowale O. Owoseni, Kim H. Åstrand, Zilethilwe Z. Steinbach
Blekinge Tekniska Högskola
Informatics Department
Karlskrona, Sweden
{adow10, kihb03, zzst09 } @student.bth.se

Abstract

The main objective of this paper is to provide a context for understanding the symbiosis between design science and natural science; discuss the IT research framework designed by (March & Smith, 1995) *and apply it to the Socrates article by* (Flensburg, 1980).*We shall first place the scope of this article within one or more of the 16 cells in the March & Smith framework and give motivations why. Furthermore, critical analysis of the article shall be undertaken based on the guidelines as prescribed by* (Henever et al, 2004) *to determine the strength and weakness of the article. Seven guidelines have been proposed by* (Hevner et al, 2004) *to assist researchers in evaluation and understanding effective design research in information systems. These guidelines are what we shall use to understand and evaluate the Socrates article as well as judge the weakness and strength of the article.*

1. Introduction

Research involves a systematic approach to an investigation with the aim of solving a problem. Therefore suitable research methods are needed to guide the investigation. The design science approach provides a suitable and comprehensive framework for the design and the analysis of artificial phenomena such as organizations or information systems. It defines the research subjects and the methods applied to the study subject in order to systematically enhance the body of knowledge. The motivation for the (March & Smith, 1995) article came about as an attempt to recognise the importance of both design and natural science. Disciplines involving Information systems seemed to be caught in the middle in the aforementioned paradigms of scientific research. This middle ground that IT researchers found themselves in caused a division of interest and difficulty in reaching a consensus as to what constitutes genuine scientific research in this field. March and Smith proposed that the two scientific areas of difference do not have to be at logger heads with each other but rather argued the legitimacy of both because they potentially feed off from each other.

2. IT Research

There are two paradigms of scientific interests in IT – descriptive and prescriptive research (March & Smith 1995, P.252). The descriptive research can be derived from natural science and behavioural research, while prescriptive research is related to design science. In this section, we shall expound on the two scientific interests to better understand the March & Smith IT research framework.

2.1 Descriptive Research

Descriptive research is a knowledge-producing activity corresponding to natural science whose aim is to understand the nature of IT. Wikipedia describes descriptive research as statistical research that answers the questions who, what, where, when and how (Natural Science, 2011). Hevner et al put it eloquently by further stating that this perspective of research *"seeks to develop and justify theories that explain or predict organizational and human phenomena surrounding the analysis, design, implementation, management, and use of information systems.* (Hevner et al, 2004)". Fig 2.0a demonstrates the aforementioned statement in relation to the behavioural research bubble.

2.2 Prescriptive Research

Prescriptive research aims at improving IT performance and corresponds to design science (March & Smith. 1995, P.252). The idea of design science can be attributed to papers by (Simon, 1996), in which he states that "it *is possible to create a science of the artificial as an analogue to natural science*" (Simon, 1996).In prescriptive research, progress is not achieved until existing technologies are replaced by more effective ones. Design science attempts to create things that serve human purposes while natural science tries to understand the reality. By applying and producing knowledge of tasks or situations, design scientist can create effective artefacts. This paradigm of research consists of two basic activities – build and evaluate. Building is the process of constructing an artefact for a specific purpose. Evaluation, on the other hand, is the process of determining how well or not so well the artefact performs in the given environment.

In reference to fig 2.0a, you will note that the creation of these artefacts depends on the behavioural theories which are applied in design research.

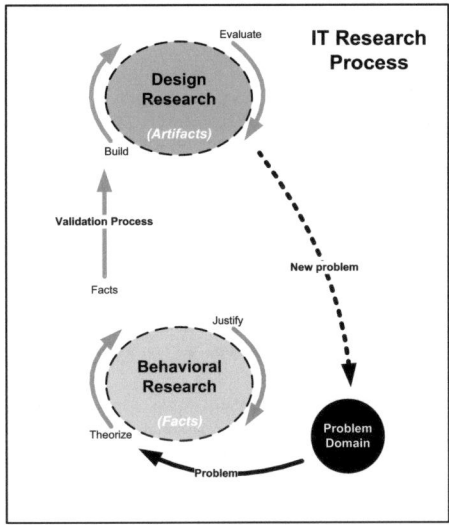

Fig 2.0a   Relationship between design research and behavioural research

2.3 March& Smith IT Research Framework

Instead of taking sides as to which of the methods of research is superior to the other when undergoing a scientific research, (March & Smith, 1995) state that "*both design science and natural science activities are needed to insure that IT research is both relevant and effective.*" March & Smith developed a framework for IT research where there is interaction between design and natural science (see fig 2.1a). The design science contributes to the framework with utility while natural science contributes with theory (March & Smith, p. 255).

Research Activities

		Build	Evaluate	Theorize	Justify
	Constructs				
Research Outputs	Model				
	Method				
	Instantiation				

Fig 2.3a IT research framework, source (March & Smith, 1995)

With reference to fig 2.1, the left column is dedicated to design research outputs and consist of constructs, models, methods and instantiations. The row on the top of the figure is based on broad types of design science and natural science research activities; build, evaluate, theorize and justify (March & Smith, p. 256). In order to describe the framework we will do a short review of the individual parts.

Constructs form the vocabulary and shared knowledge of a domain and is important in both natural and design science. Since conceptualizations define the terms used when describing and thinking about a task, it is a critical part of the framework considering reaching mutual understanding. To express the relationship among constructs, a model is used. A model is a set of propositions or statements that describe how things are. Even though natural scientist often use the term as a synonym of truth, the concern of model in this framework is utility and not truth. A method is a set of steps used to perform a task and is based on a set of underlying constructs and representations of the solution space. The natural science does not produce methods, they just use them and it is design science that creates the methodological tools that natural scientists use. An instantiation is the realization of an artefact in its environment and operationalize constructs, models and methods (March & Smith, p.258).

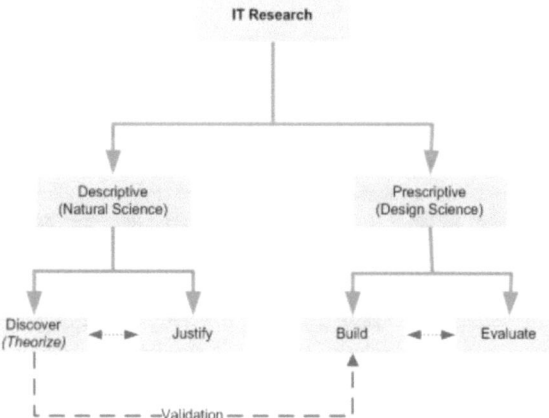

Fig.2.3b   The branches of IT Research and their relationship

In design research, the research activities are twofold: build and evaluate. Looking at figure 2.3a, build and evaluate are closely related to each other. Build refers to the construction of the artefact and demonstrates that such an artefact can be constructed. Evaluate refers to the development of criteria and the assessment of artefact performance against those criteria. By building an artefact, we can demonstrate feasibility and by evaluating the artefact we can determine if we have made any progress. After the artefact has been evaluated, it has to be determined how the artefact worked. This is done by theorizing and justifying theories about the artefacts, which you can see on the left side of the figure under natural science (March & Smith, p. 259). The theories explain the characteristics of the artifact and its interaction with the environment that result in the observed performance. The explanation must be justified, and for that evidence must be gathered in order to test the theory.

3.0 Evaluation of Socrates Article

"Transformation is only valid if it is carried out with the people and not for them"
– Paulo Freire.
The underlining factor behind any system development is the need for change and transformation that will result in better performance and organisational efficiency. According to Socrates article, it is often assumed that great user involvement will minimized resistance caused by these change and transformation; however it is imperative to understand that some requirements that are "tacit" and difficult to communicate via language (Flensburg, 1980). It is therefore not enough to just involve the users but to allow the users to develop their own system.

The high point of Socrates article is the need for an 'automated system' that is flexible enough to allow 'the *system users to develop their own sys*tem' (Flensburg, 1980, p 1). A proposal made by Flensburg describes a "*technique for user development of computerized information system*".

3.1 March& Smith IT Research Framework and Socrates Article

In the evaluation of Socrates article in reference to the March & Smith IT research framework, we concluded that it occupies the first three cells under 'Build' column of research activities as shown in figure 3.1a.

Research Activities

		Build	Evaluate	Theorize	Justify
Research Outputs	Construct				
	Model				
	Method				
	Instantiation				

Figure 3.1a Socrates article in March & Smith frame work

We based our evaluation on the following premises

- The AB technique is a novel proposition, it was new *[never done within this discipline]* and it equally demonstrates the feasibility of building computerized system with little influence from professional system developers

- The research is of great value to community of users; although the value is in the state of 'potentiality' in the sense that it is yet to be instantiated, but there is promise for positive evolution in information systems development.
- There is possibility for improvements once the feasibility of AB technique has been instantiated and gone through the designed artefact stage.
- Based on the March & Smith's argument on the distinction and relationship between Behavioural science and Design Science research, Socrates research work is a clear example of Design Research with 'build' input.

3.2 Application of the Design Science Research Guidelines to Socrates Article

Hevner et al (2004) developed a set of guidelines for conducting and evaluating design science research; the goal of these guidelines is to critically examine the relevance of the design research. It attempts to answer the following questions like – what type of research is it? Is it truly a design research? How good is the research, its conception, process and output? Has it, or can it make any meaningful impact among researchers and users at large? These are underlying research work indicators that Hevner and his colleagues seek to reveal.

As mentioned before, we shall evaluate the Socrates article under the 7 design research guidelines as proposed by Hevner et al

3.2.1 Problem relevance

Recent statistics of system development projects shows that the rate of failure is on the increase. "*According to consultant Avanade, poor system specification was the largest cause of problems, contributing to 66 per cent of cases. A lack of understanding between IT and business departments was blamed in 51 per cent of failures, while 49 per cent cited technology selection as a factor*" (Neon, 2011)

This is a clear indication that information system development require more than technical details; as a matter of fact, the need to effectively obtain '*perfect*' user requirements cannot be over emphasized because "*no system will be better than its specification*" (Flensburg, p.3). But how can system designers and developers perfectly capture these requirements?

The answer to this question is what Socrates article suggests; the article provides basic premises that should govern any requirement gathering operation. The subject of information system failure is of importance to the extent that a number of researchers are collaborating to brainstorm on a way-forward. Examples of such are the Participatory Design [PD] and Computer Supported Cooperative Work [CSCW] conferences where ideas are shared on the current findings in Human-Computer relationship. They have made it a task to bridge the gap between what the user want in a system and what the system provides. It simply buttresses the relevancy of Socrates Article [AB technique] in the quest to reduce rate of information system project failure.

Flensburg was able to clearly demonstrate the relevance and importance of the research problem with the context of Information system development.

3.2.2 Research Rigor

The research work is quite clear and precise; there was a clear distinction between behavioural research and design research. The paper laid a good foundation by establishing the boundaries between Data system and systems designer. It went further to reveal some factors [rooted in user's subconscious] that affect requirement specification; revealing the relationship between *reality*, *concepts* and *social surrounding*.

Having provided a sound base for research argument and proposition, the article extended Socrates' "*dialogues method [the act of asking trivial question in a non trivial way* "systematically to systems development field. This gave birth to AB technique, which was creatively articulated in simple and understandable terms throughout the research work with clear examples and intended outputs

3.2.3 Design as a Search Process

The author's presentation gave an impression that that there was a great deal of 'brainstorming' and root cause analysis of 'why information systems are failing'. Although system design is a design science, it has its root in behavioural science, because the systems will not exist in isolation, the systems must interact with humans [or vice versa] in order to obtain the desired efficiency and transformation.

The design process employed in Socrates article was to identify the problem, examine what is triggering the problem and then propose a novel solution - "*allowing users of computer systems to develop the systems themselves*". What an innovative and creative idea!

The author of the Socrates article is of the opinion that with AB technique, it is possible to get the linguistic and objective realities of everyone coming in contact with the computerized system; this opinion triggered the possibility of doing the construction automatically with the help of computer. A background experiment was conducted to establish the possibility of this proposition and of course, to convince the research community about the new 'reality'.

3.2.4 Design as an Artefact

For any research work to be classified as design science it must produce a variable artefact in one or more research outputs i.e.; model, method, constructs or instantiation. This artefact must be able to address an important organizational problem (Hevner et al, 2004, p. 12). How can we evaluate Socrates article against this backdrop?

The resulting artefact of Socrates article is the AB-method, Flensburg did not only provide an analytical description of AB-technique but also reveal a model that could explain it, the technique was transformed into a computer program that enhance the simulation of different 'realities'. The article went further to give details hardware/software specification of computers that can run the program.

3.3.5 Design Evaluation

Design evaluation employed in Socrates article was experimental in nature; AB-method was evaluated under controlled experiment at a Swedish company. A number of people were interviewed concerning their job; from tape recorded interviews the researcher got a formalized description of their [people's] job.

AB-method was not evaluated in terms of completeness or consistency; but on usability, performance and reliability. It is expected that the result of the evaluation will provide input into better design and clearer guidance on what works and what does not. Essentially, the author hopes that the evaluation -design loop could give birth to a complete system that is reliable, complete and consistent.

3.4.6 Research Contributions

The research work has been able to expose the salient factors that affect user requirement gathering. Two valid 'proposals' of realities were made: *1. Reality is shaped by our set of concepts* and *2. Our sets of concepts are developed in a social surrounding.* Another contribution is the design construction knowledge; it is a foundational knowledge provided by AB method and its corresponding experimental method and model.

3.5.7 Research Communication

This research work communicated to the management and technical audience. To the managers; the author provides reason why user requirements are not effectively captured, and to the technicians, Flensburg equally provides possible means of bridging the information gap through AB method. The article was detailed about its artefact design and experimental evaluation method

4.0 Conclusion

The realization of how design science and natural science can work together is demonstrated eloquently in the March & Smith (2005) article. In addition, the application of the guidelines by Hevner et al (2004) developed as a tool for conducting and evaluating design science research is intended to assist researchers to ascertain whether a given article constitutes genuine IT design research or not. The Socrates article, within the March & Smith framework, was shown to accommodate the first 3 cells under the 'build' column, suggesting that the design research article was yet be instantiated. With reference to the design research guidelines developed by Hevner et al, the Socrates article, we concluded that it constituted an effective design research in information systems. To close, we agree with Henver et al statement "*design science will play an increasingly important role in the IS profession*", however one should be mindful of the danger to overemphasise on the technological artefacts and a failure to maintain an adequate theory base (Hevner et al, 2004).

Bibliography

David et al. (2000). *Design Science: Building the Future of AIS.*

Flensburg, P. (1980). *SOCRATES - a human approach to systems developement.* Department of computer science and informatics,University of Lund.

Henever et al. (2004). Design Science in IS Research. *MIS Quarterly Vol. 28 No. 1,* , 75-105.

Hevner, A. R. (2007, November). Design Science Research: Rigorous and Relevant. National Science Foundation,University of South Florida, Florida.

March, S. T., & Smith, G. F. (1995). Design and natural science research on information technology. *Decision Support Systems* , 251-266.

Natural Science. (2011). Retrieved Jan 2011, from Wikipedia, The free encyclopedia: http://en.wikipedia.org/wiki/Natural_science

Neon, K. (2011). *High failure rate hits IT projects.* Retrieved Jan 2011, from Computing - Insight for IT leaders (eMagazine): http://www.computing.co.uk/ctg/news/1829160/high-failure-rate-hits-it-projects#ixzz1AqLDxazF

Simon. (1996). The Sciences of the Artificial.